Meet the Ferret

The ferret was domesticated several thousand years ago to help hunters flush rabbits from their holes ("ferreting out") and pursue small pests like rats and mice.

The word *ferret* is from the Latin root *fur*, the same root word that gives us the word *furtive*, which couldn't be a more suitable name for this "little thief."

The ferret's closest relatives are the European polecat, otter and skunk.

The ferret has taken up the title of third most popular companion mammal behind the dog and cat.

Ferrets live between six and ten years.

Ferrets are carnivores, which means their teeth are designed for tearing and eating meat. Their canine teeth are long and, in most ferrets, stick out beyond the lips.

The ferret has scent glands all over his body, including an anal scent gland that he can "express" in much the same way the skunk does, as a form of protection.

Ferrets come in an array of colors, including sable, chocolate, cream, cinnamon, silver and albino.

Ferrets like to sleep, often sixteen to eighteen hours a day.

Ferrets are very social animals. They enjoy the company of other ferrets and humans.

When it comes to grooming, ferrets are low-maintenance pets.

Ferrets are very curious and intelligent animals and have the ability to learn tricks and social skills.

Some characteristics of the ferret include the following: curious, likes to burrow and hide, extremely active, playful, friendly, requires training, attention and affection.

Consulting Editor
BETSY SIKORA SIINO

Featuring Photographs by
ERIC ILASENKO

Howell Book House

An Imprint of Macmillan General Reference USA
A Pearson Education Macmillan Company
1633 Broadway
New York, NY 10019

Library of Congress Cataloging-in-Publication
Data

       The essential ferret / consulting edi-
tor, Betsy Sikora Siino; featuring photographs by
Eric Ilasenko.

          p. cm.
  Includes bibliographical references and index.
  ISBN 1-58245-078-1
  1. Ferrets as pets. I. Siino, Betsy Sikora.
II. Ilasenko, Eric
  SF459.F47E77 1999   98-53978
  636.976'628—dc21   CIP

Manufactured in the United States of America
10 9 8 7 6 5 4 3 2 1

Series Director: Michele Matrisciani
Production Team: Clint Lahnen, Dennis Sheehan,
  Terri Sheehan, Chris Van Camp
Book Design: Paul Costello
Photography: All photos by Eric Ilasenko.

ARE YOU READY?!

☐ Have you decided on where to buy or from whom you will adopt your ferret?

☐ Have you prepared your home and your family for your new pet?

☐ Have you gotten the proper sup-plies you'll need to care for your ferret?

☐ Have you found a veterinarian who is experienced in treating ferrets?

☐ Have you thought about how you will train and socialize your ferret?

No matter what stage you're at with your ferret—still thinking about getting one, or he's already part of the family—this Essential guide will provide you with the practical information you need to understand and care for your new companion. Of course you're ready—you have this book!

THE ESSENTIAL

Ferret

The Ferret's Senses

SIGHT

The ferret is an animal that is often and quite accurately compared to a cat, though his eyesight is not presumed to be as sharp as that of a cat.

SOUND

His ears are remarkably sensitive, enabling him to detect trouble well before it endangers him.

TASTE

The ferret's sense of taste is highly developed. He is, in large part, motivated by securing tasteful treats.

SMELL

The ferret has a truly keen sense of smell, which helps this small predator explore any new item that catches his fancy—and everything catches his fancy!

TOUCH

The ferret's sense of touch is focused in his sensitive skin and hair, which help fuel his insatiable curiosity as he barges into any new situation.

CHAPTER ONE

Getting to Know Your Ferret

1

If ferrets could talk, they'd most likely say things like, "Everything on the floor is mine!" "What's this?" and "Look at me!" Ferrets are hypercurious bundles of energy when they are young and retain this energy level throughout most of their lives. They balance this intense energy with deep, relaxed sleep. Ferrets have their own personalities, and each will have his own favorite toys, games, treats, hiding places and sleeping spots. They are very intelligent and will quickly learn what they can get away with. They will even try to train you to do what they want.

FERRETS NEED TRAINING AND SUPERVISION

How you train, socialize and treat your ferret will go further in determining his personality than anything else. The more love and affection you show your ferret, the

Ferrets are extremely social and enjoy interacting with people and other animals.

Ferrets have personalities of their own.

more he will show toward you and the friendlier he will be toward others. Ferrets are smart animals who will learn the limits you set, but if you don't set limits they will make up their own.

Ferrets are dependent on us, their owners, for everything from food and shelter to love and attention. They are truly domesticated animals who need human intervention in order to survive. Scientists describe the behaviors of the ferret species as juvenile, which is common in domesticated species. They no longer have the instincts to take care of themselves outside a human environment.

FERRETS LOVE COMPANY

Ferrets are very social animals. They enjoy the company of other ferrets

and humans. Because ferrets have little sense of personal space, they are usually not possessive of food and will all eat from the same bowl as long as there is plenty for all. Although they are not territorial, you will notice one of the bunch emerging as the boss, or alpha, ferret. You'll notice that when another ferret joins the group, the alpha ferret will be the one the new one wrestles with most at first.

NORMAL FERRET BEHAVIOR

Stealing and Hiding Stuff

The word *ferret* is from the Latin root *fur,* the same root that gives us the word furtive. The animal is aptly

CHARACTERISTICS OF A FERRET

Curious

Likes to burrow and hide

Extremely active

Playful

Friendly

Needs a totally "ferret-proof" environment

Requires training, attention and affection

3

named. One of the ferret's favorite activities is stealing and hiding things, thus his reputation as being a "little thief" is pretty accurate. Different ferrets have different tastes and choose

This adorable masked creature is really a thief! He loves to steal and hide your things.

to steal different things. Almost all ferrets like to steal leather (key chains, gloves, shoes). Many like to steal socks (especially dirty ones). Some like to steal plastic or rubber things. Your ferret will have his own peculiar tastes.

Regardless of what your ferret likes to steal, he'll probably find an out-of-the-way place to hide it. Most ferrets hide food "for later." It has nothing to do with how much you feed them. If your ferret tends to steal things you need regularly (like your keys), you should probably make a note of where he keeps them.

Dance of Joy

This is the dance of the ferret. The ferret will hop about, often backward or sideways, with reckless abandon and with his mouth wide open. Bouncing off walls and furniture is common. This can frighten people who don't understand ferret behavior, but it is actually just your ferret's way of expressing how happy he is and how much energy he has.

Sleeping

Ferrets like to sleep, often sixteen to eighteen hours per day. If they are left alone in their cage with nothing to do, they will usually just go to sleep. This means that when you are ready to play with them, they will be fully recharged and ready to go. Ferrets' bodies can be especially limp when they are sleeping, so it is important to support them very carefully.

Ferrets spend sixteen to eighteen hours a day sleeping, so when they are ready to play, they mean business!

Ferret babies, called kits, sleep very deeply. Sometimes ferrets who are sick or old will sleep deeply also.

Yawning

Ferrets yawn a lot. It's very cute, and can be contagious. It comes with the territory of sleeping a lot.

Shivering

Your ferret's body temperature drops while he's sleeping, and when he first awakens he may need to warm himself up. Likewise, if your hands are cold and you pick up your ferret, he will probably shiver. It's important to note that he is not afraid, just cold. Shivering is not a fear reaction; frightened ferrets usually stay very still.

Litter Box Quirks

Ferrets have a very quick metabolism and need to both eat and use the litter box throughout the day. Often they will need to "go" within a few minutes of waking up. Most ferrets are excellent when it comes to using the litter box in their cage. To help keep your ferret on his best behavior, wake him up a few minutes before you want to let him out of the cage

for playtime. You may be able to get him to use the box before he comes out to play and thus help prevent accidents outside the cage.

Ferrets can be fussy about exactly how and where they are standing in the litter box. They often hop in and out of the litter box several times, sniff at the litter box and position and reposition before they actually use the box.

Any ferret will tell you that the proper place to poop is in a corner. Because of their quick metabolism, when ferrets have to go, they have to go. They will search for the best available corner (a ferret's bathroom motto is: "any corner in an emergency!"). To ensure that your ferret uses the litter box, place litter boxes in all of his favorite corners. If for some reason you want to discourage the use of a particular corner, try placing a food bowl or a bedding towel there. Ferrets won't poop in their food or in a good place to sleep.

After using the litter box, ferrets like to wipe their behinds on the ground, which often means on your carpeting. Although this can be a sign of parasites in a dog, it is normal behavior for a ferret. Some people put small replaceable "wiping rugs" near the favorite boxes.

Ferrets use their mouths like people use their hands. This ferret demonstrates his ability to pick up and move his toy with his mouth.

Ferrets usually understand that they are supposed to use their litter box and that not using it upsets their owners. They will sometimes go in a place they know is inappropriate (even right next to the litter box) in order to protest anything from an insufficiently cleaned litter box to having a toy taken away from them to not getting enough attention. Regardless of the reason, you must never physically punish a ferret for failing to use the litter box.

Chewing on Bad Things

Ferrets like to grab things, pull on things and chew on things. Some of these things they don't intend to eat, like rubber bands, ear plugs, sponges, paper and so on, but if a piece accidentally breaks off, they may not be able to do anything but swallow it. These pieces can lodge in their stomach or intestines and cause a life-threatening blockage (see chapter 3). It is important to note the types of dangerous things your ferret tries to chew on and keep them away from him.

Self-Cleaning

A ferret will sometimes try to get his smell "just right" by licking his front paws and using them to wipe from behind his ears down to his face. It looks like he is trying to wash his face. Actually, he is picking up ferret scent from the scent glands behind his ears and using it to improve his aroma.

Flat Ferret

When bored or while pondering what to do next, ferrets may lie down flat

on their stomachs and just stay still. It may be time for you to play with them or find them another toy.

Itching

Ferrets are very itchy animals and they scratch an awful lot. They will sometimes even stop mid-run, scratch an itch and then keep running as if they never stopped. They sometimes wake up and suddenly have to scratch somewhere.

If your ferret scratches more than usual or if you notice fur missing or a rash, there may be a problem. Consider everything that touches your ferret's skin: bedding, what the bed-

ding is washed in, dryer sheets and so forth. Try to eliminate the cause of the irritation. If the itching becomes severe or your ferret's skin becomes raw, seek advice from your veterinarian.

Fetishes

Different ferrets can fall in love with different items and become protective of them. One ferret had a plastic ball that he treated like a baby ferret. He protected it and occasionally carried it around to show it the surroundings. He sometimes even left it in the food bowl for a while to give it a chance to eat. When he was done with the ball, he placed it back in its own

This ferret lies on his stomach while deciding what to do next.

COMMON FERRET BEHAVIORS

To the uninitiated, these behaviors may seem strange. As you get to know your ferret, you will become familiar with these and many other unique activities.

Sleeping sixteen to eighteen hours a day

Yawning

Stealing and hiding objects

Shivering

Itching

Digging

special spot. If another ferret played with it, he grabbed the ball away and returned it to its spot. He even went through a phase where he would scream whenever another ferret tried to take the ball away from him.

Bottlebrush Tail

When a ferret is excited, the hair on his tail may stand on end, resembling a bottlebrush. This is sometimes a fear/anger reaction (as when fighting with another ferret), and sometimes a "what's this new stuff?" reaction (as when brought into new surroundings).

This little guy is pooped out from hours of fun and exercise!

Ferret Play

It seems that ferrets live to play. But their play behavior can be mistaken for real fighting if you are unfamiliar with what they are doing. Below are some of the normal activities ferrets participate in to amuse themselves.

WRESTLING

Ferrets need to figure out who is boss. They will play fight with each other to find out. When a new ferret is introduced, he will need to find out where he stands with each of the other ferrets. Often the larger, older ferret will grab the smaller, younger ferret by the scruff of the neck and drag him around.

EXERCISE TIME

Ferrets have a lot of energy and need to expend it by having some running-around time every day. They will get very frustrated and stressed if left in their cage for too long without a chance to run.

MOVING THINGS AROUND

Ferrets like to move things around. They can drag some incredibly heavy objects, and have an incredible amount of determination. If a boot can't fit under the couch, they will

9

keep on trying. Pushing a ball around on the floor with his nose is a fun game for the ferret, and funny to watch. Many ferrets will lie on top of small round objects and move them by scooting backward. This is a behavior the ferret inherited from his wild ancestors, who moved eggs in this manner. The ferret's wild behavior, however, is half gone as a result of domestication, and most ferrets have no clue what to do with the object once they've moved it across the floor.

Round 1: These two critters play wrestle to figure out who is boss.

DIGGING

The ferret's ancestors were burrowing animals, so ferrets like to dig into things or run their noses through them. Most ferret owners keep their plants well out of reach of their ferrets. The food bowl or litter box can be fun to "nosedive" through, and some ferrets will even try to nose-dive through a bowl of water. If your ferret throws litter and food around, he might be trying to tell you he's upset about something (like you're not giving him enough attention). Ferrets consider tissue boxes to be a great find, because the more they keep digging at them, the more tissues keep coming out. Some ferret owners keep a kiddie pool filled with clean, damp sand for their ferrets to burrow through.

CHAPTER TWO

Homecoming

WHERE TO BUY YOUR FERRET

Pet Shops

The majority of ferrets in the United States come from large breeder farms that supply the animals to pet shops. These farms routinely neuter and descent (remove the anal scent gland from) the ferret kits before they even reach the pet shops. Many of the kits sold in pet shops have

This ferret rescue shelter volunteer helps a visitor adopt a rescued ferret.

two small bluish tattoos on their ear flaps. These indicate that the ferret has been neutered and descented.

maturity before neutering her gives her the opportunity to grow with the benefit of sex hormones.

Private Breeders

There are also smaller, private breeders who sell kits directly to pet owners. Many private breeders do not neuter the kits before they sell them, recommending instead that the new ferret owner wait until the ferret is at least 6 months old (fully mature) before having this surgery performed. Sex hormones play a significant role in helping the ferret mature. Waiting until the ferret has reached full

Ferret Shelters

Ferrets are also available through a ferret shelter/rescue. Most animal shelters that take in cats and dogs do not take in or adopt out ferrets, but they might have information on how to find a ferret shelter near you. Most adoptees are wonderful animals whose original owners didn't do their research before bringing home a ferret. Few, if any, ferrets are beyond rehabilitation. They come around with love and attention. A reputable ferret shelter will not attempt to place a ferret inappropriately. You will most likely have to answer questions about your home and sign a contract in order to adopt a ferret.

CHOOSING A FERRET

It is often recommended that new ferret owners get an adult ferret as their first ferret. This depends on what your household is like and how comfortable you feel with the training of a kit.

If you've had experience training a puppy, training a kit will come relatively easily. This may influence your

FERRET HOUSING REQUIREMENTS

Ferrets can live happily in a cage provided there is plenty of time outside the cage for them to play, exercise and interact with people and their environment.

Things you'll need to provide a cozy home for your ferret include the following:

Large wire mesh cage

Bedding to place over the cage floor (no wood chips; use old blankets, towels or another soft material)

Litter box

Water bottle

Extras, like hammocks, tunnels, ramps and other architectural toys

This ferret hangs out in her hammock while waiting to be adopted from her rescue shelter.

Before you take a ferret home, spend some time playing with her and getting to know her personality.

decision regarding getting an adult versus a baby ferret. If you've never had an animal that requires socialization and training, you might want to look into getting an adult.

In choosing the right ferret for you, there are some things you should be looking for. Choose one that feels right. Ferrets have a variety of personalities, so you should play with several before deciding which one you want.

When you go to choose a ferret, you will want to hold her. When you pick her up, make sure you support her whole weight. Dangling a

ferret—particularly a bottom-heavy ferret—can put too much stress on her spine and may injure her. It is best to hold her with one hand under her "arms" and the other under her behind. Of course, it is easy to support the entire weight of a small kit, but as she gets older, you will have to be aware of how you are supporting her.

FERRET-PROOFING

Ferret-proofing is unlike proofing your home for any other animal except, perhaps, a human toddler. Ferrets interact with objects as well as people—they like to move things and make things happen. A ferret's small size allows her to get into very small spaces. Often, ferret owners set aside a room or two that their ferrets are allowed to play in. Keep in mind that ferret-proofing is never complete because your ferret will constantly be showing you new things that need to be kept out of her reach.

Since ferrets are truly domesticated animals, they can survive only a few days outside on their own. Their fearless curiosity usually gets them into trouble even quicker than that. Make sure all screen doors to the outside have sturdy, working latches. Make sure any window screens are secure so your ferret can't push them out and fall out the window. When you have visitors, make sure they know to watch out for your ferret.

One of the best starting points in ferret-proofing your home is to lie on the floor on your stomach. Look for any small holes (2 inches square) that might lead into the walls or to the outside, and block them securely. Once you've blocked off the holes near the floor, look around the room for anything your ferret could use to climb on. Some ferrets are exceptional climbers, though they are not very good at getting down.

One of the most common causes of death in ferrets is intestinal blockage. Many ferrets will eat things they shouldn't: rubber, latex, foam, plastic bags, paper, shoe insoles, foam ear-plugs. The taste of the object doesn't matter; they seem to like the chewy texture. Any spongy or rubbery item should be removed from the area where the ferret will be playing. Although some ferrets are more prone than others to eating odd objects, it is best to take the most cautious route.

Another common cause of injury and death in ferrets is getting caught

in reclining chairs or fold-out couches. If you have a recliner, don't use it when your ferret is out playing. Better still, move it to a room your ferret will not be allowed in— or get rid of it altogether.

Another danger of couches and chairs is their stuffing. Ferrets can and do find or make holes in the fabric covering the bottom of couch-es or chairs. Then they climb up inside their newfound and private hideout. This is dangerous for sever-al reasons. First, your pet might eat the stuffing, leading to an intestinal blockage. Second, if you need to get to your ferret in a hurry, you might

HOUSEHOLD DANGERS

Ferrets are indoor pets, so you won't need to worry about the danger lurking outside your house. However, there is plenty inside you need to keep your ferret safe from:

Electrical cords

Cleaning supplies

Refrigerator, stove and dishwasher

Clothes dryer

Houseplants

Reclining chairs

Ferret-proofing is a must. Her abundance of curiosity and determination make off-limits items all the more attractive to the ferret.

not be able to reach her. Third, ferrets in your couch could make a mess. To prevent this, you can nail a board or heavy wire mesh onto the bottom of couches or chairs. Of course, not all ferrets will try to get inside your couch. If you supervise your ferret's play carefully, you can prevent any damage to your ferret or your furniture.

You might bring home a ferret who likes to chew on electrical wires. The best way to avoid a tragedy is to keep electrical cords off the floor and out of your ferret's reach. If this is not possible, you can purchase a type of molding that is used to house the wires so your ferret cannot get to them. Another alternative is to spray the cords (but not the plugs!) with Bitter Apple or Bitter Lime spray. If you use the

cream, make sure you rub it in completely or your ferret might swallow a blob of it, which could make her ill. Some ferret owners wrap the cords in aluminum foil, which ferrets generally do not like to chew.

Most ferrets like to dig up plants. This is only natural, because they come from a long line of burrowing animals. Ferret owners have come up with some creative ways to help keep their plants and ferrets living together happily and safely. The first option is to move all plants out of your ferret's reach. This will work unless you have a determined climber or very large potted plants that must stay on the floor. The second option is to place large stones on top of the soil in the plant pot. This will keep your ferret from getting to the dirt. It can also weight down the pot, helping to deter your ferret from knocking it over. Third, you can securely attach wire mesh across the top of the plant pot so your ferret cannot reach the dirt. If you have a particularly persistent ferret, you might want to keep your plants in a no-ferret area of your home.

Plant digging, although messy, is not as dangerous as plant eating. Some plants are poisonous if eaten (poinsettia, for example) and should be kept away from all pets and children. If your ferret takes a liking to eating plants, treat the plant as you would foam rubber—keep it far away from your ferret.

No-Ferret Zones

Perhaps the most dangerous room in your home is the kitchen, with the laundry room coming in second. Ferrets can get under the stove, dishwasher or refrigerator. These appliances often have fans, insulation, wires or pilot lights that can cause fatal injuries to your ferret. Many well-loved pet ferrets have died because they were electrocuted under the stove or were badly cut when a fan under the refrigerator turned on suddenly. Ferrets have been known to drink cleaning solutions like

Electrical cords are a favorite attraction of the ferret. Ferret-proof wires and cords by keeping them out of your ferret's reach.

17

window cleaner. Many more ferrets have died because they fell asleep in the clothes dryer.

How do you prevent these tragedies? Make these rooms "ferret-free" zones. You can use a 3-foot high piece of stiff cardboard or a lightweight but rigid wood (e.g., doorskin or pressboard) to block the entrance(s) to your kitchen during ferret playtime. You probably don't want a hard wood barrier because you could get hurt if you accidentally kick it while trying to step over it. A baby gate is not recommended—your ferret will only use it as a ladder to get to the other side.

Use obstacles like this gate to keep your ferret from entering the "ferret-free" zones in your home.

18

Even with these precautions, get into the habit of looking through your laundry before you wash it and always check your dryer before turning it on. Ferrets like to sleep in clothes hampers. Open dryers—especially warm ones on cold days—are an open invitation. Ferrets have gotten closed in refrigerators, dryers, closets, drawers and cabinets; be aware of where your ferret is when you are opening and closing any of these. Before you sit down, check under couch or chair cushions. Check under throw rugs before stepping—that bump under the rug could be your ferret.

PROPER TOYS

Ferrets love to play and they remain playful their entire lives. Your ferret will prefer some toys to others, but be sure that whatever your ferret wants to play with is safe. Not all toys labeled for ferrets are safe for them. Many manufacturers are just beginning to make toys for our little friends, and they don't always have experience with ferrets to determine whether the toy is safe. Most sturdy, heavy rubber toys—such as those for large dogs—are appropriate.

Never give your ferret soft latex toys or spongy foam rubber toys. A ferret's teeth are designed for eating meat and can therefore tear apart soft toys easily. Your ferret will likely swallow a piece of rubber and, because a ferret's intestines are extremely narrow, she might end up with an intestinal blockage. Routinely check your ferret's toys for chewed areas. As soon as a toy is damaged—even if it's your ferret's favorite—throw it away.

Many homemade toys are greatly loved by ferrets. Most ferrets love to run through cardboard tubes, like those from wrapping paper. As long as your ferret doesn't chew on the cardboard, these can make great toys.

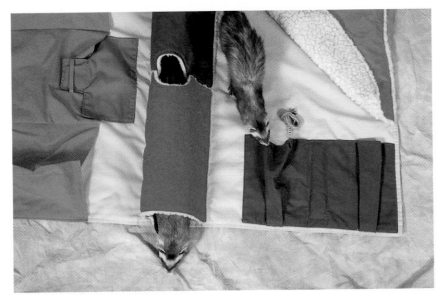

These ferrets couldn't ask for anything more as they enjoy hours of fun in their blanket complete with tubes, pockets and pouches.

SETTING UP THE CAGE

A ferret should never be kept in a glass aquarium. Ferrets need wire cages similar to those for rabbits or cats. But make sure to cover any wire mesh flooring with linoleum or bedding (towels, blankets) because ferrets should not walk on the open mesh. There are several ferret-specific cages on the market. Some are better than others. As a rule, you should make sure that your ferret has plenty of space, with separate areas for a litter box, food and water and sleeping. Depending on the type of latch on your cage, clips to keep the cage secure might be a good added safety measure.

Do not use wood chips in a ferret cage. Cedar and pine chips are treated with oils that can cause your ferret severe respiratory discomfort. There are reports of ferrets taking months to recover from the irritation and damage caused by being kept in wood chips. For the sake of your ferret's health, don't use them. Besides, ferrets are trained to use a litter box (see chapter 8), so there is no need for wood chips anyway.

A wire cage loaded with toys, tubes, hammocks, bedding, litter and food will keep your ferret safe and entertained.

Ferret Snooze Spots

Hammocks are a special favorite of ferrets. They come in many colors and styles and are available in most pet shops. Towels (make sure they aren't frayed or have loops that the ferret might catch her nails on), old sweatshirts or T-shirts, sweatpants or baby blankets are ideal for use as bedding for ferrets. For the first few days especially, check the bedding for any signs that your ferret might be eating it. Some ferrets do eat cloth. If you have a cloth-eater, try using a tightly woven fabric for bedding and leave something in the cage that is appropriate to chew.

ADDITIONAL SUPPLIES

Other items you'll want to pick up before or at the same time you get your ferret: a water bottle or dish, a food dish, litter boxes (one for the cage and at least one in every room your ferret plays in), cat litter, Ferretone or Linatone, Bitter Apple (or Lime) spray (see "Nip Training" in chapter 8), ear cleaning solution, nail clippers, shampoo (see chapter 5), a cat hairball remedy (like Petromalt or Catalax), a harness and leash and a cat carrier. You'll also need to get food for your new friend as discussed in chapter 4.

Water Bottle

Ferrets need to have fresh water at all times. It is best to equip your ferret's cage with a large water bottle, like those made for rabbits. Change the water in the bottle daily to ensure it is always fresh. When you wash the bottle, be sure to rinse away all traces of soap. If the bottle gets too dirty, get a new one.

Food Dishes

Many ferrets like to dump food dishes, mostly for fun but sometimes to make a point (such as, "Pay attention to me!"). The food dish you get for your ferret should be weighted so she can't tip it over.

Litter Box

Most ferret owners train their little friends to use a litter box (see "Litter-Box Training" in chapter 8). There are several ferret-specific litter boxes on the market. Some are designed to fit in the corner of the cage. Some have high sides for ferrets that tend to back up high into corners. Some have one low side to make it easier for your ferret to get in and

Provide a water bottle in your ferret's cage for her convenience.

21

out. This design is particularly good for older ferrets, who might not be as agile as they once were, or for small kits. Then, of course, there are plain old cat litter boxes that come in various sizes. Any of these are fine to use.

For litter, you will want something that is low-dust. Remember that ferrets are lower to the ground, and therefore closer to the litter in the box, than cats. Also, ferrets—particularly young ones—have a tendency to run their noses through clean litter. Clumping or scoopable litters are not recommended for ferrets because the litter will stick to their noses and get in their eyes. It can also stick to your ferret's fur and rear end, and when she cleans herself she can swallow it. There are several pelletized litters available that are more appropriate for ferrets. Pelletized newspaper is also good.

Leash and Harness

If you plan on taking your fuzzy friend outside with you, you will need to get her a harness and leash. The best type of harness is the H-shaped harness. A harness made especially for ferrets will fit much better than a kitten harness cut to fit. As long as you can fit a finger between your ferret and the harness, it is not too tight. Your ferret will get used to wearing the harness fairly quickly. When you put the harness on your ferret she will likely act as if it hurts her or as if she can't walk. It is just that—an act. If you loosen the harness, she'll have it off in seconds. It is very important to fit the harness onto your ferret so she can't get it off. The last thing you want is for her to get out of her harness while you're outside, so practice inside first. You can add a little bell to your ferret's harness if you want, but be aware that the bell could get caught on something. Some ferret owners leave the harness on their ferrets all

This light sable ferret never explores the outside world without being on leash and in a harness.

the time and the bell helps them know when the ferret is underfoot.

Travel Carrier

You will want to purchase a cat carrier for short trips. The size carrier you get depends on the number of ferrets you have (or plan to have). A small cat carrier is appropriate for one or two ferrets on a short trip. To prevent accidents, you should always put your ferret in a carrier when you travel by car. If you're in a car accident, your ferret is more likely to go unharmed if she is in a carrier.

A plastic grate allows good ventilation in a pet carrier.

CHAPTER THREE

To Good Health

FINDING A VETERINARIAN

Ferrets have special veterinary needs. Many ferret-specific diseases may be misdiagnosed by veterinarians without ferret experience, resulting in unfortunate consequences. Take the time to find a veterinarian with whom you and your ferret are comfortable. Don't be afraid to ask questions about how many ferrets the veterinarian sees weekly and what types of ferret medical problems he or she has treated. Look into emergency-care veterinarians who personally provide twenty-four-hour service as well.

Your new ferret kit will need to visit the veterinarian a day or two after you bring him home. During this visit, he should be checked for any parasites (like ear mites) and for overall health. He'll also receive a vaccination. Be sure to bring a stool sample so your veterinarian can check for intestinal parasites.

VACCINATIONS

If you bring home an adult ferret and you do not know or cannot find out his vaccination status, you will need to have him vaccinated. In these cases, it is recommended that the ferret receive two canine distemper vaccinations three weeks apart and yearly boosters thereafter.

The ferret should also receive a rabies vaccination.

Canine Distemper

Ferrets are susceptible to canine distemper (not feline distemper, as was once believed), a viral infectious disease that affects the respiratory, gastrointestinal and neurological systems. This disease is fatal and it is airborne, so you can bring it in on your clothes. You must vaccinate your ferret against canine distemper. Usually the breeder, whether private or one of the large breeder farms,

25

Your ferret needs a veterinarian who is experienced and comfortable with treating ferrets.

26

Keeping your ferret healthy means keeping his vaccinations current.

has given the kit his first canine distemper vaccination. A kit receives a canine distemper vaccination at 6 to 8 weeks of age and every three to four weeks afterward until he is 14 weeks of age, and then yearly boosters thereafter. Usually, your ferret will get one distemper shot at the first veterinarian visit and another shot three or four weeks later.

Rabies

Whether or not your ferret goes outside, he should be vaccinated against rabies. It may be required by law in

your area. In any event, if your ferret bites someone, having up-to-date rabies vaccinations can be reassuring and can help keep your ferret from being killed and tested for the virus. Most important, keeping your ferret's rabies vaccination current protects him if he comes in contact with a rabid animal.

NEUTERING

The vast majority of ferrets bought in pet shops come from large breeder farms that alter (spay or castrate) and descent the animals before they

Rescue shelters supply adoption tags that inform potential owners about whether the ferrets have been neutered or descented.

even reach the store. Because the surgery is performed when they are very young, there will be no physical indication that the surgery has been performed (that is, the fur will be grown in and you will not see a scar). However, ferrets from large breeder farms usually have a tattoo in one of their ears, which indicates that the ferret has been neutered. If you get your ferret from a private breeder, you will need to have her spayed (or him castrated) by the time she reaches 6 or 7 months old. The breeder should give you the information you need, and recommend a

veterinarian who can perform the surgery. If the breeder doesn't offer this information, ask.

Pet ferrets must be neutered. Female ferrets (jills) will not come out of heat on their own. Prolonged heat will lead to serious medical problems and, eventually, death. Male ferrets (hobs) cycle into "rut," which, for our purposes, can be described as something like a female's heat cycle. When a hob is in rut, he is aggressive toward other male ferrets (not people), even males that have been neutered. Also, hobs in rut have a very strong, unpleasant odor, and they can undergo dramatic weight changes and suffer anxiety if they are not bred.

EMERGENCY CARE AND FIRST AID

Animal Bites

If your ferret is bitten by another animal, put pressure on the wound and take him to the veterinarian. Tell your veterinarian that your ferret has been bitten, especially if your ferret has been bitten by an unknown, stray or wild animal. If possible, find out if the animal that bit your ferret is up to date on its rabies vaccinations.

Bleeding

If your ferret is bleeding, apply pressure to the wound and go to the veterinarian. A ferret tends to ignore pain until it is extreme, and while he may not be acting any differently, he may have internal injuries you are unaware of.

Broken Bones

If you suspect your ferret has broken a bone, try to keep him from moving around and go to your veterinarian. Often confining your ferret to a small carrier or wrapping him in a towel will keep him from moving around too much. Do not try to splint your ferret's legs. If you have stepped on or sat on your ferret, keep him immobilized (in a small carrier or wrapped in a towel) and take him to the veterinarian. If your ferret takes a bad fall or is dropped, take him to the veterinarian even if he seems all right.

Broken Tooth

A chipped or broken tooth is not necessarily a problem for your ferret. It becomes a problem if the root is exposed or if the tooth begins to decay. If you notice that your ferret's tooth is turning brown or that he is favoring one side of his mouth, take him to the veterinarian. A decaying tooth can lead to other problems, including gum disease and abscesses.

Dehydration

You can tell if your ferret is dehydrated by gently pinching the scruff of his neck. If the skin stays pinched, he is dehydrated. If the skin snaps back, he is all right. You should observe how quickly your ferret's skin snaps back when he is healthy so you will be able to tell whether he is dehydrated when he is sick. If you even suspect dehydration, contact your pet's veterinarian immediately.

Diarrhea

Because ferrets are small animals, diarrhea can become life-threatening if not treated quickly. Diarrhea can occur as a result of stress, dietary indiscretion (like eating one raisin too many), foreign body obstruction, gastrointestinal irritation, liver disease, coccidiosis or toxicity. It could also be due to a bacterial, parasitic or viral infection (see "Epizootic Catarrhal Enteritis," under "Common Diseases and Conditions," later in this chapter).

Another possible, though uncommon, cause of diarrhea is proliferative bowel disease, which occurs especially in young ferrets. The general rule is: If your ferret has more than two loose stools, take him to the veterinarian and bring a sample of the stool with you. Your veterinarian will be better able to diagnose and treat the cause of the diarrhea if he can examine the stool. Prolonged or repeated bouts of diarrhea can lead to dehydration and death. To treat dehydration, make sure your ferret drinks plenty of water or electrolyte replacer.

EMERGENCY WARNING SIGNS

If you notice any of these symptoms, get in touch with your veterinarian as soon as possible.

Severe and sudden loss of appetite

Green or yellow nasal discharge

Profuse diarrhea

Repeated vomiting

Severe itching

Dark brown or black ear wax

Lethargy

Black, tarry stools

Absence of stools

Excessive hair loss

Panting

Persistent coughing

Seizures

Electric Shock

If your ferret gets shocked as a result of chewing on an electrical wire, you should wrap him in a blanket to keep him warm and bring him to the veterinarian.

Heatstroke

This condition results from increased temperatures and is possible at temperatures above 80°F. If your ferret exhibits symptoms of heatstroke (panting, severe lethargy, limpness, seizures and, eventually, unconsciousness), you will need to decrease your ferret's body temperature steadily, but not suddenly. You can apply cool (not cold) water over your ferret, concentrating on the feet and groin areas. You can also apply rubbing alcohol to your ferret's feet only (not his whole body). Be careful not to bring his temperature too far down. Give him water if he will drink on his own. Then you should bring your ferret to the veterinarian even if he seems all right. He might need fluid replacement and further care. It is always best to prevent heatstroke. Do not leave your ferret in a car for any amount of time during spring and summer months. Keep him out of direct sunlight and make sure that he always has plenty of fresh water.

Poisoning

If your ferret drinks or eats something poisonous (including human medications, cleaning solutions, alcoholic beverages, etc.), find the container the substance was in and take it and your ferret to your veterinarian. If your ferret seems all right and ate or drank only a small amount, you can call the National Animal Poison Control Center (a nonprofit organization) at (900) 680-0000 ($20 for the first five minutes, plus $2.95 for each additional minute) or (800) 548-2423 ($30 per case; credit cards only) to find out the best way to proceed. Different poisonous substances must be treated in different ways; make sure you consult a professional.

Spinal Injury

The ferret's spine is long and allows him to twist into some unusual positions. It might look like your ferret is infinitely flexible, but he is not. Never swing your ferret around, and always support all of his weight. Even then, accidents can happen. If you suspect your ferret has a spinal injury, try to keep him as still as possible and go to the veterinarian immediately.

Vomiting

This can be a sign of a serious illness. If your ferret vomits more than once or twice and is not able to keep food down, take him to the veternarian immediately. Vomiting is one of the primary signs of intestinal block-age, which is fatal if not treated. See "Intestinal Blockage," under "Common Diseases and Conditions," below.

COMMON DISEASES AND CONDITIONS

Adrenal Disease

Hyperadrenocorticoidism most often occurs in ferrets 3 years of age or older. These are symptoms to watch for:

- Hair loss beginning at the base of the tail (not the tip) and progress-ing up the spine (some ferrets will be totally bald before the problem is diagnosed)

- Flaky, red and inflamed skin that is sometimes overly itchy (ferrets are a bit itchy to begin with, but the hormone secreted by these growths can cause excessive itching)

- Lethargy

- In females (even if they're spayed), a swollen vulva; in males, aggres-sive sexual (mounting) behavior even if they have been neutered

If your ferret has these symptoms, you should take him to the veterinar-ian. Most veterinarians will diagnose

Because the fer-ret's spine is long and allows him to twist into un-usual positions, it is important to pick up your ferret properly: Use a firm hand under the front arms and support the back feet.

adrenal disease based on the collec-tion of symptoms outlined above. The best treatment for adrenal dis-ease is surgery to remove the affect-ed gland. Ferrets that have an adren-al gland removed can go on to live happy, healthy and long lives.

Severe hair loss on the tail base of this albino ferret is a symp-tom of adrenal disease.

Blindness

Many authorities agree that ferret eyesight isn't very good to begin with. Ferrets that are blind do all right despite their limitation. It is important to be extra gentle and careful around a ferret with limited or no vision. Most commonly the cause of blindness is cataracts, though it can also be an inherited trait. A cataract has a milky white, often opaque, discoloration within the pupil. If you notice a cataract in your ferret's eye, you should bring it to the attention of your veterinarian.

Cardiomyopathy

Cardiomyopathy is the progressive deterioration of the heart muscles, and most often occurs in ferrets over 3 years old. Symptoms include difficulty waking up, the need to rest during playtime and a general decrease in activity or collapse. As the disease advances, there is coughing and difficulty breathing and increased respiration rate. Because cardiomyopathy usually occurs in older ferrets who are slowing down a little anyway, it is often overlooked. Although there is no cure

Ferrets are very adaptable creatures with a true zest for life, and they don't let a little blindness get in their way.

for cardiomyopathy, your veterinarian can prescribe treatment.

Descenting

Ferrets have scent glands all over their bodies. When a ferret is described as "descented," it means that the anal sacs have been removed. The ferret can express this gland at will, like its cousin the skunk. However, the odor from the gland is not as strong or as lingering as that of a skunk. Many ferret owners argue that descenting a ferret is unnecessary. Many veterinarians will attempt to dissuade a ferret owner from descenting an adult ferret. In general, ferrets who are neutered early in life are also descented. If you get a ferret from a breeder and wait until the ferret is 6 months old before neutering, descenting may not be necessary. The sex hormones level out as a result of neutering, which greatly reduces the productivity of the scent glands, and odor may be controlled through regular bathing and grooming.

Epizootic Catarrhal Enteritis (ECE)

This viral infection, commonly called "Green Diarrhea," "Green Slime" or "The Greenies," affects the lining of the intestine, which causes profuse mucous diarrhea. Often, the diarrhea varies from bright to olive green. Diarrhea of any kind is a serious matter in ferrets because they are small and can become dehydrated quickly. ECE is very contagious. It is transmitted via direct contact, but you can also carry the virus on your clothes to your ferret. Researchers believe ferrets shed the virus (remain contagious) for at least six months after the episode. The only way to prevent your ferret from getting ECE is to keep him away from any other ferrets or ferret owners. If you go to a place where there are ferrets or ferret owners (like a ferret show), you risk bringing the virus home to your ferret. Keeping your ferret isolated is the best way to prevent ECE. Some people in the ferret community believe that treating it like an inevitable childhood disease is the best approach, exposing the ferret while he is young and better able to fight the virus. ECE causes a long-lasting immunity following exposure. However, some ferrets may be more prone to getting diarrhea whenever they are sick after they have had ECE.

If your ferret becomes sick with ECE, you will have to treat it aggressively. Make sure your ferret continues to drink and eat. At the first signs, with veterinary approval, start giving your ferret an electrolyte replacer, such as Pedialyte.

If you notice your ferret becoming dehydrated, you will need to bring him to the veterinarian to have fluids given subcutaneously or intravenously. Because ECE is a virus, it has to run its course. The best you can do for your ferret is make sure he stays hydrated and continues to get some nutrients. ECE is a more serious concern in older ferrets or otherwise ill ferrets.

If you suspect your ferret suffers from any ailment, don't hesitate to call your veterinarian.

Gastrointestinal Ulcers

Stomach ulcers in ferrets can be very dangerous if left untreated. Take your ferret to the veterinarian if your ferret grinds his teeth (a sign of abdominal pain); has black tarry stools (a sign of blood in the stool) or soft, poorly digested stools; is lethargic; vomits or goes off his food. If your ferret has abdominal pain, he will likely eat less or stop eating, which will make him weak. Ulcers can lead to internal bleeding, which can cause anemia. If left untreated, the ulcer can cause hemorrhage and death.

Hairballs

Ferrets like to groom themselves and their friends. This can lead to hairball problems, especially in older ferrets. To prevent hairballs, give your ferret, with your veterinarian's approval, a half-inch ribbon of a cat hairball remedy (available at your local pet store or from your veterinarian) three or four times a week during shedding seasons (ferrets change their coats in the spring and fall). Bathing and brushing are also recommended during your ferret's coat change. If your ferret is shedding

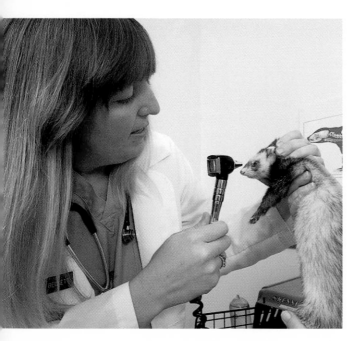

and has a dry, hacking cough, he might have some hair caught in his throat. (However, a persistent cough could be a sign of a more serious condition and should be brought to the attention of your veterinarian.) Your veterinarian might recommend that you increase the dose of cat hairball remedy to a half-inch ribbon once a day until the coughing stops. Your ferret will not cough up fur the way that cats do; therefore, it's important to make sure the fur your ferret swallows moves through his gastrointestinal tract easily. Fur that is not passed through the gastrointestinal tract can accumulate in the stomach or intestines and lead to blockages. Blockages can become life-threatening very quickly, so hairball prevention should not be taken lightly.

Hair Loss on Tail

Perhaps the most common cause of hair loss on the tail is "rat-tail," a seasonal hair loss that may be a systemic reaction to stress. Ferrets can

Grooming themselves and their friends can lead to hairball problems for ferrets.

get acne on their tails, which can lead to hair loss. If your ferret has hair loss on his tail that coincides with a coat change and that starts at the tip of the tail and is accompanied by black dots on the skin, it is probably a case of acne (but see also "Adrenal Disease," above). Wash your ferret's tail using antibacterial soap or a mild benzoyl peroxide soap daily until the black dots disappear. The hair should grow back with the next coat change. If the hair loss spreads onto your ferret's back or does not seem to improve, see your veterinarian.

Heartworm

Depending on where you live, heartworm disease can be a serious concern. Because the vast majority of ferrets are kept indoors, heartworm, which is transmitted by mosquitoes, is not a common problem in much of the United States. But if you live in an area where heartworm is prevalent—in particular, the southern United States—or if your ferret is regularly outside for long periods of time, heartworm is a very real concern. Fortunately, there is a way to prevent heartworm disease. Talk to your veterinarian about putting your ferret on medication to prevent heartworm. If your ferret is older than 6 months and has never been on heartworm preventive, you should have him tested for the presence of heartworms before starting him on the preventive medication.

Hiccups and Coughing

For the most part, hiccups in ferrets are completely normal. If your ferret is coughing, check to see that his throat is clear of any obstructions, like a piece of food or some other object he might have tried to eat. The best way to get a good clear look into your ferret's throat is to gently hold him by the scruff of his neck, which will make him yawn. Do not push the food or object further into his throat. If you can pull the object out safely, do so. If a piece of food is stuck, offer your ferret water, Ferretone or a cat laxative (like Petromalt) to help him move the object down his throat.

Influenza

Ferrets can get the same flus that you and I can get. If you have a cold or flu, avoid handling your ferret. If you must handle him, wash your hands before you do and avoid breathing directly on him. Your ferret's symptoms will be similar to the symptoms you experience when you have a cold or flu: sneezing, runny nose and eyes (clear discharge), slightly decreased appetite, lethargy and sometimes diarrhea. Influenza in ferrets tends to last longer than it does in people (up to three weeks). Although flus are usually not life-threatening, they do cause discomfort and can sometimes lead to more serious illness. If your ferret's symptoms become worse, if he stops eating, the discharge from his nose becomes yellow or greenish, or if you suspect your ferret is having difficulty breathing, don't hesitate to take him to the veterinarian. Otherwise, make sure he has plenty of water and lots of warm blankets. Make sure he continues eating and drinking and let him rest as much as he wants. And remember that you can catch the flu from your ferret as readily as he can catch it from you.

Insulinoma (Pancreatic Tumors)

The symptoms of insulinoma are often not noticed until the disease is quite progressed. The most common symptom, lethargy, can often be misinterpreted as just getting older—especially because insulinoma occurs in ferrets who are 3 to 4 years and older. One of the major problems with insulinoma is that it causes low blood sugar, which can lead to symptoms such as lethargy, disorientation, drooling, vomiting or pawing at the mouth, depression, rear-leg weakness or loss of coordination and, in some cases, weight loss. In severe cases, your ferret might have seizures resulting in jerky leg movements, vocalizations and involuntary urination. Insulinoma can be treated with drugs or with surgery. Many ferret owners choose to use both methods of treatment. If your ferret has insulinoma, you will need to discuss the best treatment for him with your veterinarian.

Intestinal Blockage

One of the most common causes of death in ferrets is intestinal blockage. This should be reason enough to fastidiously ferret-proof your home. A ferret's intestines are very narrow and can become blocked by some of the odd things he decides to eat. Basically, ferrets can and will chew on and possibly swallow anything that is springy, spongy, soft or chewy.

Some of the more common items/ substances that have been removed from ferrets are the following: foam (e.g., earplugs, cushions, foam balls, shoe insoles), rubber (e.g., soft latex toys, rubber bands, balloons), cotton, string, sponges and hairballs (hairballs are discussed above). Ferrets can also become blocked by nuts, paper or plastic bags.

Signs of intestinal blockage include vomiting, refusal to eat or decreased appetite, dehydration, absence of stool, small or "skinny" stool, straining, lethargy and depression. If you notice any of these symptoms, take your ferret to the veterinarian immediately.

Lymphoma/ Lymphosarcoma

The most common malignancy in ferrets is lymphoma, or tumors of the lymph nodes. Sometimes it can be treated and put into remission with chemotherapy, but more often it is fatal within a few months. Basically, there are few symptoms to warn of this disease until it has progressed pretty far. Some of these symptoms you or your veterinarian might see are enlarged lymph nodes, diarrhea, weight loss and weakness.

One of the reasons it is recommended that ferrets 4 or 5 years and older have a complete blood workup is so that diseases like lymphosarcoma can be detected early.

Prolapsed Rectum

A ferret might get a prolapsed rectum as a result of severe, chronic diarrhea or from descenting surgery. If you notice that your ferret's anus is protruding, red or swollen, you should have your veterinarian check it out immediately.

Tumors (Skin)

The vast majority of skin tumors on ferrets are benign. If you periodically check your ferret for odd lumps or bumps, you can catch skin tumors early, before they have a chance to spread or attach to anything below the skin. Your veterinarian can remove the tumor and have it biopsied.

Urinary Tract Infection

Ferrets occasionally get infections of the urinary tract. If your ferret is drinking a lot of water or seems to be having difficulty urinating, or if the urine is unusually dark in color, take him to your veterinarian. Urinary tract infections can be treated rather easily, but you do not want to delay treatment. These infections can progress up the urinary tract and potentially cause kidney infections.

Urine Drinking

Sometimes ferrets drink their own urine. Although it is a disturbing practice, it is nothing to worry about.

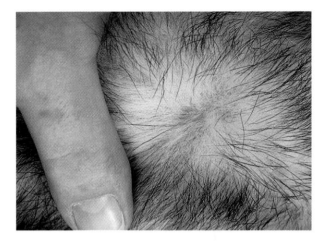

Weight Loss or Gain

Ferrets' weight can vary greatly throughout the year. They tend to put on a good deal of weight in the winter and lose quite a lot again in the summer. Ferrets have been known to go from 3 pounds at their heaviest to 2½ pounds at their lightest. Some ferrets vary more than this. If the weight loss is seasonal and coincides with a coat change, it is normal. If the weight loss or gain is sudden and your ferret's behavior has changed, see your veterinarian.

This veterinarian inspects underneath the fur of a ferret and finds a mass cell tumor.

CHAPTER FOUR

Positively Nutritious

as the first ingredient. Foods that list corn or grain as the first ingredient will not provide proper nutrition.

NUTRITIONAL NEEDS

Because ferrets are strict carnivores, the food you choose for your ferret must have some form of meat as its first ingredient. Most quality ferret foods on the market list poultry, poultry meal or poultry by-products

Protein

For years, ferret owners fed their little friends high-quality kitten food (growth formula) because it has a high meat protein content. Many owners still feed high-quality kitten food because it is more readily available, and in some cases less expensive, than ferret food. Some ferret enthusiasts believe that kitten food is inappropriate because it is not designed specifically for ferrets. However, others argue that some ferret foods were formulated before animal nutritionists knew much at all about the domestic ferret's needs. This is not a problem with the newer foods

*Selected cat foods
make good daily
diets for ferrets.*

41

formulated specifically for ferrets. Certainly ferrets have thrived on kitten food for many years, and it is better than feeding a poorly formulated ferret diet.

In any case, you should never feed dog or puppy food to your ferret. Ferrets, like cats, require added taurine, which dog foods do not contain. Taurine is vital to the health of your ferret's eyes and heart. Under no circumstances should you feed your ferret a vegetarian diet. To do so will risk her health.

Fat

Animal fat is another important ingredient in a proper ferret diet. Ferrets get their energy from fat, and will eat enough food to fulfill their energy needs. That means that they will eat less of a food that has high fat content and more of a food that has a lower fat content. Food manufacturers have to make sure that there's enough protein, vitamins and nutrients within the amount of food the ferret will eat. If the percentage of fat in the food is high, the nutrient levels must also be high for the ferret to get a balanced diet. Ferrets, like most other animals except humans, will eat only enough to fulfill their energy needs. Most will not overeat.

Fat is also important to the health of your ferret's coat and skin. If you notice your ferret's coat becoming rough or her skin becoming dry, she might benefit from some extra fat in her diet. There are several fatty acid supplements available that you can give her.

Supplements

As a rule, if you feed your ferret a high-quality food, you do not need to give her vitamin supplements. Of course, you might want to give some vitamin supplements occasionally. Also, if your ferret is ill or under stress, she can benefit from any of a number of vitamin supplements on the market designed specifically for ferrets. One of the most popular types of supplements is an oil-based fatty acid coat and

Believe it or not, fat should be a part of your ferret's diet. Fat aids in keeping your ferret's coat and skin healthy.

This ferret loves to drink her vitamin supplement, which keeps her skin and coat shiny and hydrated.

43

skin vitamin supplement (such as Ferretone), which is similar to Linatone, a supplement for cats or dogs. There are also vitamin pastes, such as Ferretvite or Nutrical, that ferrets generally regard as treats. It is wise, however, to consult a ferret-savvy veterinarian before supplementing your pet's diet.

FEEDING YOUR KIT

Ferrets do not necessarily need soft foods unless they are ill or very young. Hard, dry food helps keep your ferret's teeth clean. When you first bring home a kit, you will need to soften the food by adding a little water. A young ferret's jaws are not strong enough to break up the hard food. At this early age, you could offer a high-quality canned kitten food in addition to the moistened kibble, but it is not necessary.

It is important that your kit get used to the taste of the kibble, since this is the diet she will eat when she is an adult. As she grows, she will gain the strength she needs to eat hard food. She is usually ready to eat only hard food at the age of 12 to 14 weeks.

44

Ferrets are not territorial and therefore enjoy eating their meals together from the same dish.

CHANGING YOUR FERRET'S DIET

Never change your ferret's diet suddenly. The best way to switch from one food to another is to do it over the course of about ten days. Start by filling your ferret's dish with a mixture of 10 percent of the new food and 90 percent of her current food. Decrease the percentage of old food by 10 percent as you increase the percentage of new food by 10

percent each day until your ferret's bowl is 100 percent new food.

Gradually switching will help your ferret become accustomed to the new flavor and will give your ferret's body time to adjust to the different nutrient levels. One of the most common side effects of changing foods is diarrhea. No matter what brand you're switching to or from, your ferret will likely have a few loose stools. This is a normal reaction to the dietary change. Once your ferret's body has adjusted, her stool should return to normal. Make sure she drinks plenty of water so she doesn't become dehydrated.

TREATS

Giving your ferret treats is a good opportunity to create a bond between you and your pet. Often, the only time a young ferret will sit still long enough for you to hold her is when you are giving her a treat. But remember, no treat should keep your ferret from eating her regular food. The most important thing to remember about treats is that they are just that—treats. Anything you feed your ferret that is not her regular diet should be kept to a minimum.

FOODS YOUR FERRET SHOULDN'T HAVE

Ferrets, like children, tend to most like the things that are worst for them. Sugar or anything with sugar in it, for example, is well-loved by our fuzzy friends. But ferrets can't

45

Giving treats is a great way to create a lasting bond with your ferret.

Nothing can stop a ferret from getting to some treats. This light sable ferret will crawl through a tunnel to get some.

process sugars very well—not even natural sugars. Keeping your ferret off the sweets is your best bet. Ferrets also tend to like alcoholic beverages, which contain very high amounts of sugar. You should never allow your ferret to drink beer or wine or anything with alcohol in it.

More "don'ts": nuts, dairy and chocolate. Ferrets can't digest nuts, and if your ferret swallows a large enough piece, he can end up with an intestinal blockage. Some ferrets

love peanut butter, which is okay as a treat, as long as it is smooth peanut butter, not chunky and is offered sparingly. Dairy foods will cause diarrhea in ferrets. Chocolate can be toxic to ferrets and other animals. Although ferrets have stolen and eaten a bit of chocolate with no adverse effect, it is not worth the risk.

Basically, try to remember that ferrets are small, and even small amounts of things like sugar, alcohol or dairy foods can be hard for them to digest and may make them sick. Stick to the nutritious treats; your ferret will thank you for it. Stick to the following guidelines, consult your veterinarian if you have any questions, and feeding your ferret should be an easy task.

- high animal protein and fat content

- food available all the time

- plenty of fresh water

- supplements if needed

- treats should be healthful and kept to a minimum

47

CHAPTER FIVE

The Best-Tressed Ferret

Good grooming is not just a matter of making your pet look pretty. Keeping your ferret's ears and teeth clean and his nails trimmed will help keep him healthy and happy. You should set up a regular grooming routine for your ferret that includes bathing and brushing (especially during shedding season), nail clipping, ear cleaning and checking teeth for tartar buildup.

Close attention to coat, nails, ears and teeth helps you keep your ferret looking and feeling his best.

BATH TIME

How often you should bathe your ferret depends on who you ask. Some owners swear by bathing once every two to four weeks. Others insist that ferrets need not be bathed unless they actually get dirt on them (from, say, rolling in the mud or digging in a just-watered plant). Whatever works best for you is fine, but don't bathe your ferret more often than every two weeks. Frequent washing strips away essential oils, leaving your ferret's fur coarse and his skin dry, and generally making him very uncomfortable.

There are several ferret-specific shampoos on the market you can use to wash your ferret. You can also use a baby-safe shampoo or, as some ferret owners recommend, an all-natural peppermint soap bought at a health food store. If your ferret has fleas, you can use a flea shampoo that is safe for kittens. Never use flea dips on your ferret; they are too harsh.

Bathing your ferret can be easy. You can bathe him in a kitchen or bathroom sink, in the bathtub or in any basin. Make sure the room is fairly warm and there are no drafts.

Your ferret's body temperature is normally 101° to 102°F, so a "lukewarm" bath can feel pretty cold to him. (That's why he races up your arm and tries to leap off of you—it's cold!) The water should be about as warm as a bath for a child—not too hot, but comfortable. Warming the shampoo bottle in the bath water beforehand can add to your ferret's comfort. Don't overfill the sink. The water should reach only up to your ferret's shoulders, so he can stand in the water without feeling that he has to swim. Keep in mind that while some ferrets love the water, many only tolerate it, and some are simply terrified. Be patient and offer treats for good behavior. The more pleasant you make your ferret's bathing experience, the easier it will be on both of you.

When wetting down your ferret, make sure you support his weight. Apply the shampoo carefully and avoid getting it in his eyes. After lathering up, make sure you rinse. And rinse. And rinse. Leaving shampoo residue on your ferret can make his fur rough and his skin dry, which can be very uncomfortable for him.

Make sure your ferret has a clean place to dry off. Ferrets tend to head for the dustiest, dirtiest places to rub against to get dry, undoing any

washing you have done. A dry bathtub or other confined area filled with towels for your freshly washed ferret to burrow through is a fun way to dry off. You might want to warm the towels in the clothes dryer first—but don't let them get too hot. Some ferrets will tolerate being blown dry. If you choose to do this, be careful. Choose a warm—not hot—setting, keep the blow dryer at least 12 inches away from your ferret, and move the blow dryer frequently to prevent burns. Wherever or however you dry your ferret, make sure the room is warm and has no drafts.

BRUSHING YOUR FERRET

Particularly during shedding seasons (spring and fall), you may want to brush your ferret to help remove loose fur. (Ferrets get hairballs. More on those in chapter 3.) Choose a brush for cats or kittens, keeping in mind that your ferret's fur is not as long as some cats' fur. Try a medium-bristle cat brush on your ferret.

CLIPPING NAILS

Keeping your ferret's nails trimmed is an important part of his grooming

When brushing your ferret, be sure to use even pressure—some ferrets are a bit ticklish and will squirm to get away.

51

program. Your ferret will need to have his nails clipped about every two weeks, some more often, some less. Ferrets tend to wear down their back nails quicker than their front nails, so you may need to clip the nails on the front paws more frequently.

The Clipping Procedure

The easiest way to clip your ferret's nails is to put a drop or two of Ferret-one (or other "lickable" treat) on his belly. While the ferret is licking the treat, he will not notice that you are clipping his nails.

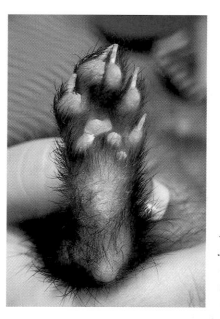

Regular nail trimming will prevent your ferret from getting his nails caught on carpeting or bedding.

52

This good boy calmly endures a nail trim.

You can use a cat nail clipper or a human nail clipper to trim your ferret's nails. Some ferret owners find that human clippers tend to crush the nail before cutting it; making sure the clippers are sharp minimizes this concern. Other ferret owners feel that cat clippers obstruct the view of the nail. Use whichever type of clipper you feel most comfortable with.

Once you have chosen the type of clipper you will use and have prepared your ferret's belly, you're ready to start trimming. While your ferret is licking the treat, gently spread apart the toes on each foot, in turn, and clip the nails. Try to clip the nail so the tip will be parallel with the floor. Avoid clipping the quick (the pinkish-red vein inside the nail), because it will bleed. If you do clip it by mistake, put styptic powder on the nail. If you have no styptic, you can put the ferret's nail in cold water or run the nail across a bar of white soap to stop the bleeding. You may want to resume the nail clipping later in the day to give your ferret some time to calm down.

CLEANING EARS

Cleaning a ferret's ears can be a real challenge, but it must be done. If you don't clean your ferret's ears, they become a breeding ground for mites. Left untreated for a long period of time, ear mites can cause severe damage to a ferret's eardrums and the delicate bones of the inner ear, leading to infections and possibly deafness. If you suspect your ferret has ear mites (a dark brown or black discharge that looks like coffee grounds, scratching at ears), have him examined by your veterinarian. Keeping your ferret's ears clean will also minimize ear wax and prevent the odor associated with wax buildup.

The hardest part of ear cleaning is that ferrets usually don't like it. You can use any ear-cleaning solution that is considered safe for kittens. Many of the all-natural ear-cleaning solutions are fine as well. Keep in mind that the inside of your ferret's ears are sensitive and must be moistened in order to be cleaned. Do not use a dry cotton swab.

A good method is to wet down one end of a cotton swab with ear-cleaning solution, swab the ferret's ear (never go into the ear canal, go only as far as you can see) and use the dry end of the swab to remove dirt, wax and excess moisture. Ferrets have a little "pouch" at the back of the ear that can collect a good amount of dirt and wax. Make sure you clean this pouch thoroughly. It is not the ear canal, so you can slip the cotton swab in and out without causing any damage. And always, always be gentle.

CLEANING TEETH

Your ferret's teeth accumulate tartar just as any other animal's do. Unfortunately, many owners overlook their ferret's dental health. Gum disease—characterized by red, inflamed gums—can lead to severe discomfort and infection. A decayed or abscessed tooth can make your ferret go off his food and lead to serious infection and even death. It is important that your ferret always have hard food to help keep his teeth clean. In addition, your veterinarian should periodically perform a complete dental exam and service on your ferret, including removal of tartar on the ferret's teeth

53

FERRET GROOMING ESSENTIALS

Shampoo

Cat or kitten brush

Cat or human nail clipper

Cotton swabs

Ear-cleaning solution

Gauze

and above the gum line. Most ferrets need this full procedure after they reach about 3 or 4 years of age.

Tartar is a gray or greenish discoloration on your ferret's teeth. Usually it is seen first on the back teeth. If any of your ferret's teeth are a brownish color, there is a possibility of decay. Have your vet check it out as soon as possible.

If you start when your ferret is young, you can get him used to having his teeth cleaned fairly easily. Although nothing takes the place of a professional tooth cleaning, there are some things you can do to help keep your ferret in good dental health. Between tooth cleanings, or from the time your ferret is young, you can use a cat toothbrush or wrap ordinary gauze around your finger and "brush" his teeth on a weekly basis. It will

Frequently inspecting your ferret's teeth for inflamed gums, tooth decay and tartar will help ensure good dental health. Say Aah!

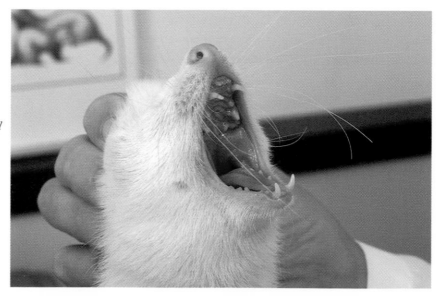

take some time for your ferret to get used to this, so be patient and gentle. Always offer a reward for good behavior.

Never use human toothpaste on your ferret; the ingredients (especially fluoride) are poisonous when swallowed, and ferrets can't spit it out. Besides, most ferrets hate the smell and taste of it. If your ferret will tolerate it, you can use a toothpaste specially formulated for cats. The more important part of brushing is the abrasiveness of the gauze, which helps take off the tartar while it is relatively soft, so toothpaste is really not needed. Your ferret might tolerate the brushing better if you put a drop of Ferretone or Linatone on the gauze.

Close attention to coat, nails, ears and teeth helps you keep your ferret looking and feeling his best. It also helps keep pesky ferret odors at bay. Grooming your ferret gives you an opportunity to recognize potential problems and prevent them before they start. In short, keeping your ferret clean makes him a pleasure to be around.

CHAPTER SIX

A Matter of Fact

So, now that you've learned how to choose a ferret, how to feed, house and groom her, what exactly is a ferret? A ferret is a small, furry, carnivorous (meat-eating) mammal.

Her teeth are sharp enough to tear meat, her body flexible enough to burrow through the smallest opening, yet the ferret is among the most domesticated of animals in the world.

The ferret has earned the place of honor beside the dog and cat in the laps of thousands of humans.

While she is loving and playful, she'll rob you blind, as she is a thief and loves to steal your things and hide them away for herself.

Many people mistakenly believe that the ferret is the wild North American Black-Footed Ferret or another kind of wild animal. In fact, the ferret is a domesticated animal, not a wild animal that has been tamed or raised in captivity. The ferret was domesticated several thousand years ago to help hunters flush rabbits from their warrens (holes) and pursue small pests like rats and mice.

In some European countries and Australia, the ferret still works at

CHARACTERISTICS OF THE FERRET

- Curious about everything
- Alert
- Innate concern for master/family
- People-oriented
- Mischievous
- Quick learners
- Exuberant greeters

Ferrets are quiet animals, for the most part. Many will make a kind of chittering-type noise that sounds like "dook, dook, dook" when they are excited or playing.

FERRET LANGUAGE

Male ferrets are hobs and female ferrets are jills. A castrated male is a gib and a spayed female is a sprite. Names for groups of animals often come from observations about the behavior of those animals. It is not surprising, then, that a group of ferrets is called a business.

"ferreting out" rabbit warrens for hunters who set nets to catch the fleeing rabbits. But here in the U. S. the ferret has retired from the working life and taken up the title of third most popular mammal companion.

In this role, the ferret performs many equally important functions. The ferret is curiosity in a fur coat. She is playful, highly inquisitive, fearless and friendly. The ferret has a sense of humor. She is intelligent and resourceful. Her shape is elegant and her energy is boundless. A ferret is exuberant, affectionate and athletic (though a bit less than graceful). Above all, the ferret is simply adorable.

THE BASIC INFORMATION

Male ferrets are called hobs and females are called jills. A castrated male is called a gib and a spayed female is called a sprite. Baby ferrets are called kits. Females can be a little more fidgety than males. As males get older, they are more likely to turn into lap ferrets than females— but there are really no absolutes.

Hobs and gibs are up to 50 per-cent larger than jills and sprites. Hobs are usually between 3 and 5 pounds at maturity, while jills are usually be-tween 1$\frac{1}{2}$ and 3 pounds. Ferrets neu-tered when they are very young may not grow as big as those neutered after they reach 6 months old.

Life Span

Ferrets live between six and ten years. They have been known to live to be 12 years old, but more commonly they live to 7 or 8 years. Ferrets are considered to be geriatric by the time

This 9-year-old light sable ferret beat the life-span odds. Ferrets, on average, only live seven or eight years.

FERRET FACTS

- There are an estimated 5 to 7 million pet ferrets in the U.S. today.

- A ferret's life expectancy is six to ten years.

- Ferrets were probably domesticated by Europeans who used them for hunting rabbits. The first ferrets came to the United States over 300 years ago on ships in which they were used for rodent control.

they're 4 years old. Although genetics plays a large part in the longevity of ferrets, the care they receive plays a large role as well.

Vocalization

A ferret will hiss as a sort of warning to another ferret who's annoying her. When ferrets play together (and they can play rough), they tend to make a good deal of noise. Sometimes it sounds like they're hurting each other, but when you separate the two ferrets they go right back to play fighting. If a ferret is hurt, there is no mistaking the shriek.

Meat Eaters

Ferrets are carnivores, which means their teeth are designed for tearing

and eating meat. Their canine teeth are long and, in most ferrets, stick out beyond the lips.

Ferret Odor

All mustelids have a characteristic musky aroma. The ferret has scent glands all over her body, including an anal scent glad that she can "express" in much the same way the skunk does, as a form of protection. However, the odor from a ferret's anal scent gland is not as pungent or as lingering as the odor from a skunk. Except in rare cases, a ferret will not express her anal scent gland unless she is frightened or feels threatened. For the most part, it is impossible to tell whether or not a ferret has been descented unless she has recently expressed the scent gland.

Ferrets in heat (jills) or rut (hobs) do smell, but because it is highly recommended that pet ferrets be neutered (females can die from complications of prolonged heat), you will not have to worry about that odor.

Markings

You should choose your ferret based on her personality, but seasoned ferret owners know that "I don't have that color" is a good excuse to get another ferret.

Considering that ferrets are little thieves, one of the most appropriate markings on a ferret is the mask. Masks can be a band across the eyes or shaped like a **V**. Some are clearly delineated and others sort of trail off into the other color on the ferret's face. Often the guard hairs, the longer hairs in the coat, are a different color from the undercoat, which is the softer, shorter fur. Ferrets' coat colors often change slightly from season to season, and sometimes the shape of the mask will change slightly as well.

Ferrets also often have markings or patterns. One of the most common

Ferrets come in an array of colors. Pictured here are ferrets in (1) silver, (2) dark silver, (3) sable, (4) light sable and (5) albino.

FERRET'S COLORS

Ferrets come in many different colors and have different markings. Sable (dark brown) and chocolate (light brown) are the most common. Another common color (actually lack of color) is albino. Albino ferrets are white with red eyes. Other colors include champagne (cream-colored), cinnamon (reddish) and silver (light gray).

patterns is the Siamese or color point pattern, where the legs, tail and mask (referred to as "points") are considerably darker than the body, and the mask is shaped like a V. Another common pattern is the solid or self pattern, where the body and points are the same color. Additionally, there's the standard pattern, in which the points are only a little darker than the body.

This Siamese fer-ret's legs, tail and mask are considerably darker than her body.

A panda ferret.

The panda ferret pattern is characterized by a white head, bib and feet. There is no mask on a panda. Blaze (also called badger or Shetland) is characterized by a white stripe on the top of the head, with white fur at the knees and feet or toe tips. Blazes have white bibs and often have dark smudgelike markings around their eyes. When a ferret is called a silver mitt, it means she is silver and has four white feet—mitts are simply white feet.

THE FERRET'S RELATIVES

The ferret's closest relatives are the polecat, weasel and mink. Other relatives are the ermine (winter coat) or stoat (summer coat), skunk, otter, wolverine and the endangered North American Black-Footed Ferret (BFF). The ferret is the only domesticated member of the family.

IS THE FERRET THE RIGHT PET FOR YOU?

Ferrets are extremely social and love to spend quality time with their families.

After addressing the basics, it is now time to ask yourself if the ferret is indeed the right pet for you. It is important to be sure before you bring one home.

Do You Mind the Smell?

As we mentioned above, ferrets have a special smell. In fact, all animals have their own particular odor, and ferrets are no exception. It isn't that ferrets smell more than other animals, but that they smell different from what most people are used to. Some people do not like the ferret's musky aroma. Others think it's earthy and pleasant.

Do You Have the Time and Attention to Give?

You cannot get a ferret and leave her in her cage all the time. Ferrets must get exercise every day for several (two or more) hours. They are very social and need companionship. If you will not be able to spend a lot of time playing with your ferret (which means getting on the floor and playing), you should consider getting two ferrets, or none at all.

Can You Make the Necessary Adjustments to Your Home?

Ferrets like to burrow. They like to hide and sleep in dark places, under blankets and in clothes baskets. Some ferrets are diggers. If you are not willing to make some adjustments for ferret behaviors, a ferret might not be the best pet for you.

Ferrets are loving, affectionate, funny, entertaining animals who are willing to adapt to your lifestyle. Are you willing to meet them halfway? They'll rearrange their sleeping hours (all sixteen-plus of them) so they can play when you're available. Will you in turn make the time to play with them?

Can You Afford the Expense?

Ferrets need a good ferret food or high-quality kitten food, which can be a bit expensive. Can you afford that expense? Can you afford the yearly vaccinations and potentially serious illnesses your ferret might get when he is older? Some ferret behaviors can be exasperating. Do you have the patience to look after a perpetually inquisitive animal?

CHAPTER SEVEN

Ancestry

Not very much is known about the history of the ferret. There are stories and myths, but not very much hard evidence about where these little animals come from or when, exactly, they were domesticated. The only sure thing is that an animal fitting the description of a ferret appears in some ancient writings.

THE FERRET'S ANCIENT ORIGINS

So when was the ferret domesticated, and by whom? Some say the Egyptians domesticated the ferret a few hundred years before they domesticated the cat. This is based on an Egyptian hieroglyphic depicting an animal that looks like a ferret. Some argue that the animal could be a mongoose, which has a shape similar to a ferret's and which was commonly used in Egypt to keep homes free of snakes and other pests. It is also argued that because ferrets are particularly susceptible to extreme heat, which is common in North Africa, it is unlikely that the animal in the hieroglyphic is a ferret at all.

It isn't until Aristophanes's time (450–425 B.C.) that there are written accounts of an animal that fits the description of a ferret or a domesticated polecat. In 350 B.C., Aristotle used the same word Aristophanes had used to describe an animal that was probably a truly domesticated ferret.

By Roman times, the ferret was most certainly domesticated. The use of ferrets in flushing rabbits from their holes (called "ferreting") was widespread by this time. By the end of the Roman Empire, ferreting was common throughout Europe, primarily practiced by peasants.

WORKING HERITAGE

Ferrets have done their share of work. They will not only chase rabbits from their warrens, but they are also excellent mousers and ratters. In ancient times, the Phoenicians likely used ferrets on their ships to keep them free of rats and mice. They were used throughout Europe for centuries to control rodent problems in homes and barns. During the Revolutionary War, ferrets were used on American ships to control rodents. Ferrets have

The word ferret, derived from the Latin word for thief, is an appropriate name for this little criminal.

67

Although the origin of the ferret is basically unknown, there are accounts of an animal that fits the description of a ferret in ancient writings.

also been used to run wire through narrow tubing in aircraft.

THE FERRET'S ANCESTORS

Figuring out how the ferret evolved is not as simple as you might think. Usually archaeological evidence helps scientists piece together the route of evolution of domesticated animals from their wild ancestors. Because many of the physical characteristics

(that is, bones, skulls, etc.) of the ferret's closest relatives are hard to distinguish from others in the family, it is nearly impossible to determine where one species ends and the other begins.

The ferret's scientific name is either *Mustela furo* or *Mustela putorius furo*, depending on which theory you follow. In either case, the word *furo* means thief, an appropriate title for an animal who steals and hides the things he treasures. *Furo* is from the same Latin root as the word *furtive*, which shows that the ferret was aptly named.

It is a widely held belief that the closest ancestor of the ferret is *Mustela putorius*, the European polecat. Those that ascribe to this theory refer to the ferret as *Mustela putorius furo*, meaning that the ferret is a subspecies of the European polecat. The theory is supported by the similarities between the two animals, including their having the same number of chromosomes and similar colorings. The fact that they can breed with each other and produce fertile offspring further supports this theory. It is important to remember, however, that these two are not the same species, despite their similarities.

FAMOUS FERRETS

Ferrets have appeared in various paintings throughout history. There is a portrait of Queen Elizabeth I

In Europe, ferrets were used by peasants to flush rabbits out of their holes.

The European polecat, Mustela putorius, *is widely considered the closest ancestor of the ferret. Take a quick glance, and you might mistake this young girl's ferret for a cat!*

70

with one of her albino ferrets. Ferrets also appear in paintings by Domenico di Bartolo *(Pope Celestinus III Grants Privilege of Independence to the Spedale)* and Leonardo da Vinci *(Lady with Ermine).*

Queen Elizabeth I was not the only famous person to own a ferret. Some other famous ferret owners past and present include James Doohan and his wife Wende, Donna Rice, Dick Smothers and Dave Foley.

CHAPTER EIGHT

On Good Behavior

Ferrets are very intelligent animals, and if you don't train them, they will train you. Ferrets can learn not only basic social skills, like using a litter box and playing gently with humans, but also some fun tricks like sitting up and rolling over. Teaching your ferret good social skills is a must. An untrained ferret is like an untrained dog—unpleasant and potentially harmful. You would not let a puppy do as she pleases; don't allow your ferret to do so either. Even though ferrets are small, they are fast and strong and can play very rough.

The key to teaching a ferret anything is consistency and patience. If you are not consistent in your treatment of your ferret, she will take it as a sign to do as she pleases. This is especially important in teaching your ferret how to play with people. Keep in mind that any training must be done in the spirit of love.

NIP TRAINING

All baby animals nip. Young animals (even small children) tend to interact with their environment using their mouths. Young animals also teethe. Everyone knows puppies need to be taught that nipping is unacceptable behavior. The same is true for ferrets.

Keep in mind that, in most cases, ferrets nip far less after reaching adulthood (at approximately 6 months of

Ferrets respond exceptionally well to training when they are treated kindly.

age) than as kits. Also remember that when your ferret is teething, you will need to offer her an appropriate chew toy. Hard rubber dog toys work especially well at this stage. Don't punish your ferret for trying to teethe; she is, after all, only a baby.

During this time, you can start to teach your ferret the proper way to play with humans. Owners have had success using Bitter Apple spray. When the kit is awake and in the "play" mode, try spraying the Bitter Apple on your hands and play with her. When she nips at your hands, she'll be repelled by the taste and should soon decide it's not fun to nip the offensive-tasting human hands.

You might have a ferret that doesn't respond to Bitter Apple or Lime. Another useful tool in deterring nipping is scruffing. If your ferret grabs you with her teeth, immediately grab her by the scruff of the neck, look right into her eyes, and say sternly, "no" or "ouch." Unless you communicate with her, she won't know she's hurting you: The exact same nip on another ferret is considered play. When ferrets play with each other, they let each other know what acceptable limits are. It is the ferret owner's responsibility to "explain" to the ferret that the nipping hurts and that there are better ways of communicating and playing with people. Remember that your ferret isn't trying to hurt you; she is trying to play with you.

The key to nip training is consistency. You can't allow a nip sometimes and not others. It will only confuse your ferret. A method not recommended is hitting your ferret on the nose. In most cases, you won't hurt her. Instead, she'll think you're playing (ferrets can be tough animals!) and won't understand why you're angry. If you do hit her hard enough to let her know she has hurt you, you've probably hit her way too hard. Besides, hitting can make your ferret frightened of you and can actually make her bite more. A ferret who believes hands are things that hurt her will try to protect herself from any hand that comes near her. Instead, be patient with your ferret. She will learn.

LEARNING TO LICK

Of course, teaching a ferret that hands taste bad can also make her avoid hands altogether. After each session

73

Consistent, gentle and loving training will make your ferret well-liked.

with the Bitter Apple, you need to teach your ferret that hands are friendly and nice to lick. Use Ferret-one (or any "lickable" treat) to help teach your ferret that, although biting is bad, licking can be nice. After the kit has worn herself out a bit, hold her and offer the treat in the palm of your hands (making sure to wash all the Bitter Apple off your hands first). She licks it and begins to learn that licking humans is nice (it tastes good). Eventually, your ferret will understand that biting is bad and licking is good. Tired ferrets are less likely to nip and less likely to

struggle and squirm while being held. It is easier to create positive learning sessions by holding the ferret when she is already inclined toward better behavior.

HOLDING YOUR FERRET

Ferrets are energetic and playful, but you want to hold your little ball of fur. How do you get your ferret to relax in your arms? It is best to start with a sleepy ferret. Try to make the experience as pleasant as possible. Offer her a treat. If you get your ferret to associate treats and comfort with being held, she will want you to hold her. Be aware, however, that some ferrets like cuddling more than others, and males tend to be a little less rambunctious than females. Kits are so full of energy when they are awake that they are unlikely to tolerate being held at all. Be patient with your ferret. Let her run herself down before you try to hold her. As ferrets get older, they are more prone to being "lap ferrets."

If your ferret nips you when you try to hold her, don't put her down. She will have you trained in no time: "Every time I nip you, you will put

Lap time with your ferret is easier after she has had plenty of exercise.

me down so I can play." Instead, gently scruff your ferret and say, "no." If you must put your ferret down, put her in her cage. Try not to reward bad behavior with playtime.

"TIME OUT"

Because ferrets love to play, using a "time out" approach when they misbehave can be particularly effective. Some ferret owners keep a cat carrier handy for when a ferret plays too rough with them. This is especially useful if you have more than one ferret. The ferret in the carrier can see the other ferret playing nicely outside the carrier. When the ferret in the carrier calms down, she can come out again.

TRAINING YOUR FERRET TO COME

A ferret can have a very short attention span when she wants to. When she's in new surroundings, she is unlikely to respond to you. But sometimes new surroundings are dangerous and you need your ferret to respond immediately. It is always worthwhile to train your ferret to come to a

75

Because ferrets love to play, "time out" in a crate can be an effective training method if play turns rough.

specific type of sound, like a special squeak toy, a bell or other loud sound that your ferret can hear from a distance. Make sure that every time you use this sound, and she comes, that you give her a favorite treat. She should have no doubt that she will be rewarded for coming to this sound. If your ferret is ever lost inside or outside your home, you can use the special squeak toy or bell to find her.

WALKING ON A LEASH

If you choose to take your ferret for a walk, you will want to have your ferret on a harness and leash (see chapter 2 for information about leashes). Although some ferret owners have been able to get their ferrets to walk nicely on a leash, most are more likely to take their ferrets for drags rather than walks. You will probably follow your ferret as she explores more than you will have her heeling at your side. That's fine. It is difficult to teach your pet to stay nearby when there's a whole world of new things to sniff. With a ferret, the function of a leash is to keep her from wandering off, getting distracted and forgetting to come back.

Use a leash to prevent your ferret from wandering off, getting distracted and forgetting to come back.

LITTER-BOX TRAINING

One of the great things about ferrets is that they can be trained to use a litter box. A mother ferret will often teach her kits to use a litter box if the kits are left with her long enough. But because most ferrets are separated from their mothers before this is done, you will have to help your ferret figure it out. Ferrets naturally seek a corner to use as a bathroom. When you see young ferrets in a cage, you'll notice that they usually use a corner of the cage as a bathroom. You can use this natural behavior to your advantage in teaching your ferret to use the litter box.

Your ferret's cage should be equipped with a litter box of your choosing. Put only between a half-inch and an inch of litter in the box. If you put too much litter in the box it becomes a place for your ferret to play instead of to do his "business." Because ferrets don't cover their waste like cats do, they really don't need much litter on the bottom of the box. It is best, particularly during the training stage, to leave a bit of waste in the litter box at all times so your ferret remembers what the box is for.

77

Show your ferret to the closest litter box when she starts to seek a "bathroom" corner.

Ferrets usually have to use the box within a few minutes of waking up. When you wake up your ferret for playtime, make sure she uses the box before you let her out to play. It's also a good idea to let her get some food and water before you take her out to play. Ferrets can be clever, and many a ferret has faked using the litter box in order to get out of the cage for playtime. Don't be fooled.

Once she has used the litter box, you can let her out to play. Allow her only a small area to play in at first. This will keep a small kit from being overwhelmed by huge new things all at once. It will also help you to litter train her. Every half hour or so during playtime, place your ferret in the litter box in her cage. If she uses it, praise her lavishly. If she doesn't, let her continue playing. Anytime you notice your ferret backing into a corner, quickly move her into the litter box. Vigilance is the key to training your ferret to use the litter box. Once your ferret realizes what the litter box in the cage is for, you and she are ready to increase the size of the play area.

At this point, you might want to add a second litter box at the far end of the play area. Remember to put

some of his waste in the new litter box. If your ferret prefers a particular corner within her play area for her bathroom, place the litter box in that corner. She is more likely to use the litter box if she chooses where it belongs. Again, watch your ferret as she plays, and if she begins to back up into a corner, put her into the nearest litter box. If she goes into the litter box on her own, give her lots of praise and attention. If you want, you can give her a treat. The only problem with offering a treat is that your ferret can fake using the box to get the treat. You could end up being trained by your ferret in no time.

Continue increasing the size of her play area until she is litter-box trained in the entire area she will usually have run of. If she experiences a setback, go through the procedure again until she gets it right. Because a ferret's intestines are short, when she gets the urge to go to the bathroom, it means now. If the litter box is too far away, she will look for the nearest corner. For this reason, you must have at least one litter box in each room your ferret will be allowed to play in. Some large rooms might need two litter boxes. Again, you might want to let your ferret choose the corner(s) where her litter box will be. Many ferrets do well with going in the litter box, but most ferrets are never 100 percent reliable. Either way, you must never, ever, physically punish a ferret for an accident or any setback in her litter-box routine.

CHAPTER NINE

Having Fun with Your Ferret

Ferrets are fun. That's why they make good pets. They remain as playful as kittens their whole lives. Entertaining your ferret can be entertaining for you, too. You can play all sorts of games with your ferret, teach him to do tricks and go places with him.

LEARNING TRICKS

Because he is very smart, your ferret can learn to do tricks. Ferret owners have taught their little friends to stay on their shoulder, roll over, sit up and many other types of tricks.

The principle for teaching a ferret tricks is basically the same as it is for teaching a dog: Reward the desired behavior. Make sure the reward is something your ferret likes and that is not bad for him. The key to teaching tricks is to use patience and many short training sessions.

COMING TO HIS NAME

Many ferret owners teach their ferrets to come to their names. Some ferrets learn not only their own names, but the names of other ferrets. One of the keys to teaching your ferret his name is consistency. Whenever you speak to your ferret, you need to use his name. Whenever you hold your ferret or give him treats, repeat his name over and over. Help him to associate the sound of his name with something pleasurable.

To get your ferret to come to you when you call him might take some time. You will want to start in a fairly small room or corner of a room. Say your ferret's name over and over and whenever he wanders over to you, give him a treat. Eventually, he will associate his name with coming to you to get a treat. Many ferrets will come running to the sound of a squeak toy. This can be used as the call signal or in conjunction with the call signal you want your ferret to learn.

SIT UP AND BEG

Since ferrets tend to reach up to get to things they like, teaching them to sit up for treats is not very difficult. Some ferrets have even been known

This ferret receives a raisin as a reward for coming when his name is called.

81

Eventually, your ferret will sit up even when you don't offer him a treat.

to sit up in response to hand signals! It's best to work with your ferret when he's calm or after he's had a chance to play a bit. Find a place where there are few distractions so he is more likely to pay attention to you. Use a treat that your ferret really

likes but that doesn't take very long for him to eat. Try breaking up a treat into smaller pieces. This way you will be able to get him to do the trick several times in the span of five or ten minutes, before he gets distracted.

Start by crouching or kneeling far enough away from your ferret (about a foot) to prevent him from leaning on you when he reaches for the treat. Then show the treat to your ferret so he knows what the reward is. You might want to let him sniff it in case his eyesight isn't very good. Hold the treat up over your ferret's head. If he tries to lean on you, gently push him back and try again. Whenever he successfully sits up without trying to climb on you to get to the treat, give him the treat. Go through this procedure in five- or ten-minute sessions over the course of several days.

You can also teach your ferret to sit up on command (whether or not you give him a treat). Every time you hold the treat above your ferret's head, say the word "up" or any other word you want him to associate with doing the trick. It is best to use a one-word command. After several sessions, your ferret will begin to sit up whenever you say the word. If you have a ferret who can't hear, you will have to use a simple hand signal instead of a word. Try moving your index finger in an upward motion. At first, hold the treat in the same hand you use to make the motion. Eventually, he will start to sit up in response to the finger motion alone.

ROLL OVER

For this trick, you'll need to prepare in the same way as for sitting up: Let your ferret play a bit first, find a quiet spot with few distractions, and use a treat that your ferret likes and that he can eat quickly. Be aware that some ferrets don't like being rolled over, and they will struggle against you. If your ferret seems distressed or upset, perhaps this isn't the trick for him. Teaching your ferret to roll over is a little more complicated and may take longer than teaching him to sit up.

First, show your ferret the treat and say "roll over" while gently holding him by the shoulders. Roll him all the way over and give him the treat. Do this several times during a five-minute training session. Your ferret will probably be a little confused and might become distracted. Be patient. You will probably need to do this a few days in a row until your ferret becomes comfortable with you rolling him over. Once he allows you to roll him over easily, he's ready for the next step.

Everything is exactly the same as the first few days, except that you will be rolling over your ferret only three-quarters of the way, allowing him to do the last bit of the roll himself. Whenever he successfully completes the roll, give him the treat. Once he learns this, go to rolling him only halfway over, then only one-quarter. Finally, you should be able to simply nudge his shoulder to get him to roll over. Your ferret might grasp the entire concept at any point during the training, or he might require more time. Practice makes perfect with this trick. The more you work with your ferret, the better he will learn.

While you are teaching your ferret to roll over, you can use various commands to communicate with him. You can use a voice command, you can simply show him the treat or you might want to make a circle motion with your finger (especially if your ferret can't hear).

83

OTHER TRICKS

Ferrets love to hide things, especially leather, shoes and dirty socks. Here's a fun trick you can show your friends that isn't really a trick at all. Make sure you try this on a friend who doesn't know that ferrets are creatures of habit when it comes to hiding things. Explain to your friend that your ferret is very smart and that he will put things where you tell him to. Most people will say, "of course he can," while thinking that you are just biased and maybe a little crazy. Then give your ferret something to hide, like a sock or a leather glove, and tell him to put it away. Watch your friend's amazement as your ferret stashes the item. To really impress your friends, choose an item your ferret usually puts in the same place (like a sock that always goes under the chair or a special toy that always goes behind the couch), and tell your ferret to put the item where he usually puts it. Your friends will think your ferret actually understands what you're saying. Try it.

GAMES TO PLAY WITH YOUR FERRET

Ferrets love to play with other ferrets and with you. Over time, you and your ferret will make up games to play with each other. Some of the games ferret owners play with their pets are tug-of-war and tag. You could also hang a ball from a string attached to a stick (like a fishing pole) so your ferret can jump up and bat at it with his paws. Some ferrets particularly enjoy chasing and being chased by their owners. Any time you are playing with your ferret, keep in mind that he is small and loves to get under your feet. The more you play with your ferret, the more he will come to you when he wants to have fun. So get down on the floor with the little guy and enjoy yourself. Odds are your ferret will enjoy it, too.

FUN MATCHES AND FERRET SHOWS

Many local ferret clubs hold fun matches and ferret shows to help support their educational efforts and area shelters, to educate fellow ferret owners and to have fun. The shows usually take place March through June and September through November. Sometimes you can find a notice regarding ferret shows in local papers or at local pet stores. Many

ferret shows are listed in *Modern Ferret* magazine or other publications.

Fun matches consist of entertaining contests like tube races, bag escapes or costume contests. These are designed as events to bring ferret owners together for socializing and fun. There are usually vendors selling ferret-related items that you can't find at your local pet store.

Often, more established ferret clubs hold ferret shows. These are similar in concept to cat and dog shows, but on a smaller scale. Ferrets compete for championship titles based on genetics and care/grooming. These are sometimes highly competitive shows, with ferrets from long lines of champions being entered by private breeders. There are several show sanctioning organizations, each with its own set of standards. If you decide you'd like to show your ferret, you should consider the

Your ferret will be even more willing to play with you if you get down on his level.

various groups and their standards and choose the one that best suits your own beliefs.

Ferret shows can be very exciting events. There are always vendors selling anything from basic cage supplies to unique craft items. Often private breeders will have kits for sale. Many clubs also include vaccination clinics at their shows. Ferret shows are also a great place to see all the different colored ferrets there are.

SHORT TRIPS AROUND TOWN

Since ferrets are small and can easily fit in a pocket, many people bring their ferrets with them on short trips around town. But if you will be going places where your ferret will not be welcome, leave him at home. Don't create a situation where you have to leave your ferret in the car, especially during summer months.

When traveling by car, you should put your ferret in a pet carrier, even if it is only a short trip. Never let your ferret run loose in your car. Ferrets have gotten crushed beneath clutch and brake pedals, they've leaped out of sun roofs and gotten lost inside holes in the dashboard. Besides,

what would happen if you had a car accident? A pet carrier is a wise investment that makes traveling safer and easier for you and your ferret.

Ferrets are relatively portable pets. Smaller "travel" cages can be equipped with all the comforts of ferret home and taken on the road. Many ferret owners adapt medium or large size cat or dog carriers as ferret travel homes. A small litter box can be put in as well as food dishes and a water bottle. A neat trick to create more space in a molded plastic carrier is to remove the top and fit a piece of fabric between the top and bottom halves of the carrier, creating a second story/ hammock area. Secure the fabric with the screws that fasten the top to the bottom of the carrier. Alternatively, you could purchase a small wire cage for ferret travel.

Many ferret owners who travel by car on vacations bring their ferrets along with them. Remember that ferrets on vacation still need exercise. When giving your ferret playtime in a strange house or hotel room, make sure you ferret-proof an area for him or keep him on a leash during play/ exercise time. Always supervise your ferret's playtime when you are on the road.

Many hotels will allow your ferret to stay in the room with you as long as you keep him caged. Call ahead to check with any hotels or motels where you might be staying. If you are traveling to another state, it is a good idea to make sure that ferrets are legal in all areas you travel through. Some states require you to get a permit just to pass through with your ferret.

Your ferret will give you years of joy and love. Playing with your ferret and involving him in your leisure time not only gives you an opportunity to be a little silly, but it also helps you and your ferret have a more solid and enjoyable relationship. The more time you spend playing with your ferret, the more he will enjoy spending time with you. And isn't that why you have a ferret in the first place?

CHAPTER TEN

Resources

BOOKS

Bell, Judith A., DVM. *The Pet Ferret Owner's Manual.* Rochester, NY: Christopher Maggio Studio, Inc. and Miracle Workers, 1995.

Bucsis, Gerry and Barbara Somerville. *Training Your Pet Ferret.* Hauppage, NY: Barron's, 1997.

Fox, J. G. *Biology and Diseases of the Ferret* (2nd ed.). Philadelphia: Lea & Febiger, 1998.

Jeans, Deborah. *A Practical Guide to Ferret Care* (2nd ed.). Miami: Ferrets Inc., 1996

McKay, James. *The Ferret and Ferreting Handbook.* Swindon, Wiltshire: Crowood Press, 1994.

Morton, E. Lynn. *Ferrets: A Complete Pet Owner's Manual.* Hauppauge, NY: Barron's Educational Series, 1985.

Winsted, Wendy. *Ferrets in Your Home.* Neptune City, NJ: TFH Publications, 1995.

PUBLICATIONS

FERRETS USA.
Fancy Publications Inc., 2401 Beverly Blvd., Los Angeles, CA 92718.

MODERN FERRET. Crunchy Concepts, Inc., P.O. Box 1007, Smithtown, NY 11787

NATIONAL FERRET ORGANIZATIONS

National organizations will not only provide information regarding ferrets, but can also refer you to a club or shelter in your area. Write to each of these organizations to find out which one is right for you.

AMERICAN FERRET
ASSOCIATION (AFA)
P.O. Box 3986
Frederick, MD 21705
www.ferret.org

FERRET FANCIERS CLUB (FFC)
713 Chautauga Ct.
Pittsburgh, PA 15214

LEAGUE OF INDEPENDENT
FERRET ENTHUSIASTS (LIFE)
9330 Old Burke Lake Rd.
Burke, VA 22015
www.acmeferret.com/life

LEGION OF SUPERFERRETS
NATIONAL CLUB (LOS)
P.O. Box 866
Levittown, PA 19058

NORTH AMERICAN FERRET
ASSOCIATION (NAFA)
P.O. Box 1963
Dale City, VA 22193

S.T.A.R.* FERRETS (Shelters that
Adopt and Rescue Ferrets)
P.O. Box 1714
Springfield, VA 22151
www.netfopets.com/starferrets.html

UNITED FERRET ORGANIZATION
(UFO)
P.O. Box 606
Assonet, MA 02702

FERRET LEGALIZA-TION ORGANIZATIONS IN CALIFORNIA

As of this writing, ferrets are illegal in
California. These are the two groups
working to change the law.

California Domestic Ferret Association
(CDFA)
P.O. Box 1868
Healdsburg, CA 95448

Ferrets Anonymous (FA)
P.O. Box 3395
San Diego, CA 92163
www.caoutlaws.com

FERRETS ON THE INTERNET

Below are some of the resources available on the Internet.

The Ferret Mailing List (FML) – To sub-
scribe to the FML, send an e-mail
asking to be added to: <ferret-request@
cunyvm.cuny.edu>

**The Ferret Frequently Asked Questions
(FAQ)** – To receive a copy of the Ferret
FAQ (©Pamela Greene), send an e-mail
to: <listserv@cunyvm.cuny.edu> with the
following message: SEND ANSWERS
PACKAGE FERRET.

Ferret Central (with links to many
other ferret-related Web sites) – <http://
www.optics.rochester.edu:8080/users/
pgreene/central.html>

Usenet Groups – rec.pets, alt.pets.ferrets

Modern Ferret on the Web – <http://
www.modernferret.com>

OTHER RESOURCES

The National Animal Poison Control
Center (a nonprofit organization) provides
around-the-clock service by veterinarians.
They will make follow-up calls as needed.
Call (900) 680-0000. Charges are $20
for the first five minutes, plus $2.95 for
each additional minute. Or call (800)
548-2423, which charges $30 per case,
payable by credit card only.

YOUR ESSENTIAL *Ferret* INFORMATION SHEET

Tear me out!

Put a picture of your Ferret
in this box

Your Ferret's Name ______________________

Identifying Features ______________________

____

Date of Birth ______________________

Your Ferret's Veterinarian ______________________

Address ______________________

Phone Number ______________________

Medications ______________________

Vet Emergency Number ______________________

Additional Emergency Numbers ______________________

Favorite Foods ______________________

Favorite Toys ______________________

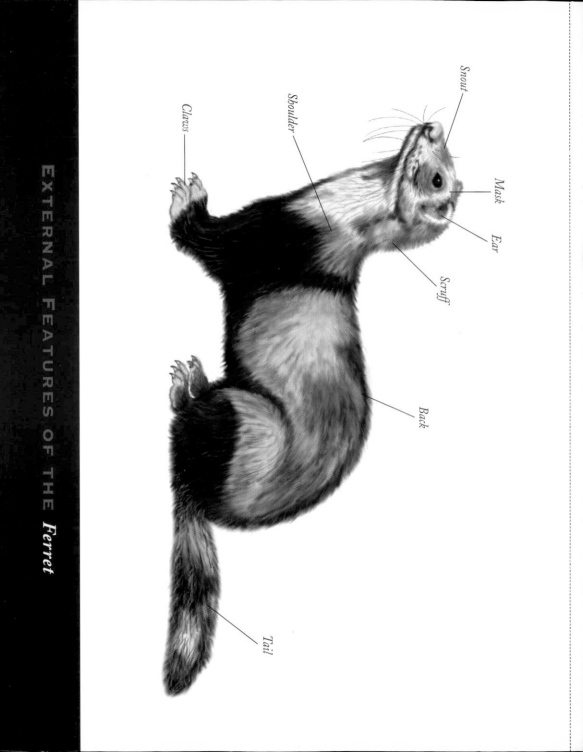

Snout

Shoulder

Claws

Mask

Ear

Scruff

Back

Tail

Owning a ferret is rewarding and fun! Get all you need to know about feeding, housing and caring for your pet's health in *The Essential Ferret*. Special features include professional color photos and expert tips on how to make your ferret a wonderful addition to the family. Learn how to have a great relationship with your pet with *The Essential Ferret*.

ISBN 1-58245-078-1

HOWELL BOOK HOUSE
MACMILLAN · USA
Find us online at www.mgr.com
Design by Paul Costello